# GUIDED**PRACTICE** ROUTINES**FOR**GUITAR
## FOUNDATION LEVEL

Practice with **125** Guided Exercises in this Comprehensive 10-Week Guitar Course

## LEVI**CLAY**

FUNDAMENTAL**CHANGES**

# Guided Practice Routines For Guitar – Foundation Level

**Practice with 125 Guided Exercises in this Comprehensive 10-Week Guitar Course**

ISBN 978-1-78933-409-8

Published by **www.fundamental-changes.com**

Copyright © 2023 Levi Clay Alexander

Edited by Tim Pettingale

**www.fundamental-changes.com**

Over 12,000 fans on Facebook: **FundamentalChangesInGuitar**

Instagram: **FundamentalChanges**

For over 350 Free Guitar Lessons with Videos Check Out

**www.fundamental-changes.com**

# Contents

# Introduction

Practice is the bane of every musician – even more so for the beginner. We all know that we have to practice in order to get better, but at the same time, *what* do we practice? And *how long* should we practice for?

I think this issue arises from the fact that, in the early stages, practice is a faith-based premise. We're told that if we do something over and over, we'll get better at it. While that may be true, we have no real way of knowing if we'll definitely get the results we want, or if we're just wasting our time.

The solution is not just knowing *what* to practice and for *how long*. We need to know WHY we're practicing something. Knowing what our goals are, coupled with a deep understanding of our personal struggles in music, will enable us to work out what we need to do to overcome them and make progress.

Secondly, I've always found it hard to practice without veering into playing. What do I mean by that? We need to make a clear distinction between *practice* and *play*.

Playing is fun, it's the end goal, it's the reason we practice, but it's not always an efficient means of progress. If you have limited time in which to get better, practice is the skill of meeting your needs with relevant exercises that will achieve your goals as efficiently as possible. The problem with efficiency, however, is that it can be boring!

You'll quickly learn that practice is two things: a means of overcoming your physical/mental struggles with the instrument, and a lifelong battle with yourself. So, we need to reframe practice. I think about my time spent practicing like going to the gym. If I'm enjoying being in the gym, then I'm not working hard enough. It's got to hurt and I should want to leave, because I know that will get me the progress I'm looking for. Once we start to see that progress though, practice becomes significantly easier to enjoy. Not because we enjoy the struggle, but because of the growth the struggle represents.

So, practice will make you a better musician, and to become a better musician is the reason you bought this book. This book is designed to teach you how to practice, and how to self-diagnose your problems, so that you can create your own personal routines to solve them. This book isn't genre specific, instead it covers the foundational skills every guitar player needs to become what I call a *bulletproof musician*. In other words, someone who can communicate well with other musicians; who can get on stage at a jam night and know what's going on. This book is for you if you want to be able to lead a band, teach music, play in a function/ wedding band, be a session player and make a living playing music.

So how does this book work, and how should you use it?

The idea is simple. There are 10 guided practice routines, each of which becomes progressively more difficult and introduces new ideas. You're not left to complete these on your own, however, I guide you through them on the free audio download and we play all the exercises together.

Remember the old aerobics videos your mum watched in the '80s? This isn't me telling you what to do, this is me doing the routine *with you*! Each routine is intended to last one week, and for that week I want you to play along with me every day. Each routine only takes about 10 minutes to complete, but by doing them together I'll keep you true.

I've been playing guitar for 20 years now, and piano for 2 years, and the guided practice routines I've done with my piano teacher were a game-changer for me. The motivated me to get up, get on with it, and know there was an end goal.

I don't expect you to read each chapter and automatically be able to do the exercises – you might need to devote a little time on the first day to working out how to play each of the examples. But once you have them down, you should be able to play along with me without any serious problems.

Here's one last idea for you…

Remember, don't practice until you get it right, practice until you can't get it wrong.

As a bulletproof musician, you shouldn't make mistakes, everything should be easy. Think about the tasks you do every day. Do you make mistakes when walking? Do you pour coffee over your face instead of in your mouth? These things are completely automatic because of repetition.

We're looking to develop a similar automatic response with the exercises here. Play everything in this book with control, and build up your speed over time. This is important as we're laying a rock-solid foundation here. As you begin each new week, you should feel like the work you did last week is making each week easier.

Although I had in mind that each routine would be practiced for one week, if that feels too fast, you *cannot* work on these routines for too long. If you need two or three weeks, then take it! If you get to week five and want to go back to week one for a review, do that. Do whatever you need to do to keep your confidence level high.

Good luck and please feel free to reach out if you have any questions.

*Levi.*

# Get the Audio

The audio files for this book are available to download for free from **www.fundamental-changes.com.** The link is in the top right-hand corner. Click on the "Guitar" link then simply select this book title from the drop-down menu and follow the instructions to get the audio.

We recommend that you download the files directly to your computer, not to your tablet, and extract them there before adding them to your media library. You can then put them onto your tablet, iPod or burn them to CD. On the download page there are instructions and we also provide technical support via the contact form.

For over 350 Free Guitar Lessons with Videos Check Out

**www.fundamental-changes.com**

Join our Facebook Community of cool musicians

**www.facebook.com/groups/fundamentalguitar**

Instagram: **FundamentalChanges**

# Routine One – Primer

This first routine is probably going to feel easy and, on a technical level, it should. It's a primer for the picking hand, to get you on the right path for the rest of the work ahead of you.

I'm a firm believer in the idea that the guitarist's picking hand is always the weakest point, and it's this that holds us back as we're trying to push forward. So, we're going to work on that now, to give us more control over what we play, how we sound, and how tight our rhythm is.

Beyond the technical challenges presented by the guitar, if we want to remove as many roadblocks from our future as possible, we need to train our brains as much as our hands. The brain allows us to think when playing – to look ahead, see scales or arpeggios, and tell each hand what to do; to conceptualise rhythm and conceive the sounds we want to play before we play them.

With that in mind, our learning objectives for this routine are simple:

* Drill in the subconscious, alternate motion in the picking hand

* Learn the notes of C Major on the E and A strings

* Play open chords

* Understand 1/4 and 1/8th note rhythms, and be able to read them


Once you've worked through the exercises and learned them, practice this routine along with me on the audio every day. You cannot put too much time into the alternate picking motion, so you'll never regret it.

First up, we have the "1234" exercise.

I'll say it now, I hate exercises like these! I find them inherently unmusical. Plus, when I'm playing real music, I don't use either the left or right mechanics in my actual playing.

So why do it?

The more I've thought about it, the more I've realised just how many of my students struggle with the alternate picking motion. For many, it's not automatic. If I pick eight notes, to me it's one constant motion. What I see from a lot of students, however, is eight deliberate motions instead.

It's like their brain tells their hand to pick downwards and, once that's done, there's a split-second delay before it instructs the hand to pick upwards. "Interrupting" the process like that is going to get in the way of both speed and rhythmic accuracy. We want to do away with that. Instead, our picking hand should just pump up and down unconsciously, as naturally as breathing.

How can we train our picking hand so that the motion becomes unconscious? Just by doing it a lot.

The twist in this exercise, compared to what I used to practice when I was a kid, is that we're only *ascending*. We are only putting our fingers down on the fretboard, not lifting them up. Each finger goes down and the pick hits the string. Why complicate things with, *finger comes up, pick hits the string*? We'll get to that! But here we are focusing on a single idea: *finger goes down, pick hits string*. It's simple, but it's also hard work.

On the audio track, you'll notice that I instruct you to control your dynamics. Think more like a pianist here; pianists are always concerned with the dynamics of a passage of music. The guitar is an extremely dynamic instrument too. It can be played softly or loudly, and we want to develop that control. So, when I tell you to play quietly, make it whisper quiet, and when I ask for it loud, dig in!

**Example 1a:**

Now your picking hand is warmed up, let's do some work on the mind.

My system of fretboard visualisation is based on chords. If you can "see" a chord, then you can see a pentatonic scale, or an arpeggio, or outside sounds, or whatever… around it.

To be able to visualise chords in this way, you need to be able to see the root notes on which the chords are built. I do this using only the low E and A strings. All my chords are built from root notes on those two strings, which reduces by about 60% the amount of work my brain has to do, compared to what would be required if I was searching for root notes on all six strings.

We'll start by playing the notes of the C Major scale (C D E F G A B C) on the low E string.

As you're performing this exercise, make sure you say the pitch of the note out loud. This isn't a fingering exercise – you're training your brain to automatically know that the note A is located at the 5th fret, and the note C is at the 8th fret, and so on.

**Example 1b:**

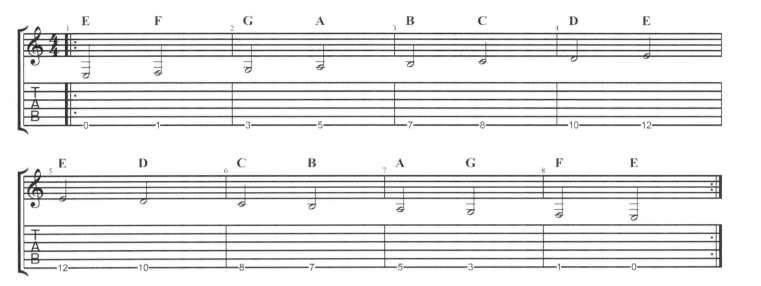

Now repeat the same exercise, but on the A string.

As you play examples 1b and 1c, also consider where these notes fall in relation to the fret markers on your guitar.

**Example 1c:**

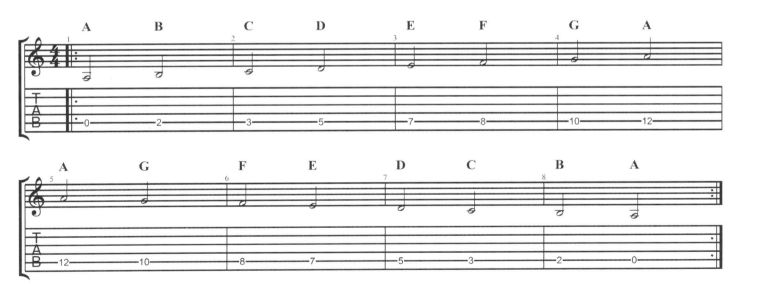

Next, it's time to get those fingers moving a bit more by playing the five open chords C, A, G, E, and D.

To keep the exercise easy, it's written so that you play the root note of the chord first, followed by the full chord. This gives your fingers plenty of time to catch up and move between chords.

**Example 1d:**

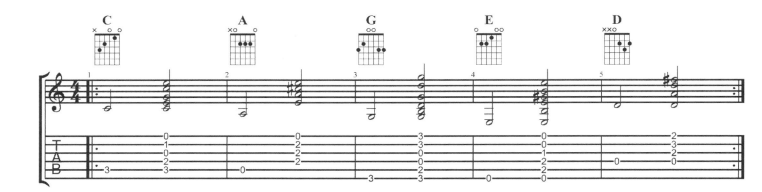

Now let's move on to some single note playing.

We're not worried about theory here; the goal is to get the fingers moving and the picking hand alternating. That's the key – drilling the alternate picking motion.

Before you begin playing, your picking hand should *already be moving* in time to the beat. Down, up, down, up.

I think of this as getting the engine started before the starter gun goes off. This is a great habit to get into, because it will help to get your timing right. But it will also hopefully train out the bad habit, which many of my newer students have, of picking the strings however they feel. We are doing away with that – it's alternate picking or bust! Keep the down-up-down-up motion going and the fretting hand will sync to it.

Pick this E Minor Pentatonic scale until both the motion and timing are effortless.

**Example 1e:**

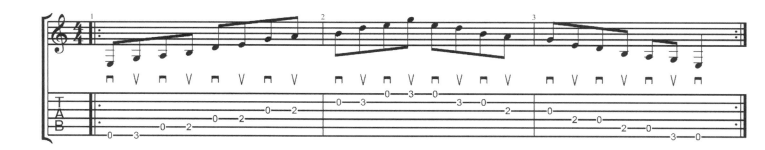

Now let's apply that picking hand motion to an open position C Major scale.

The focus here is more technical than intellectual, so let's begin there. As you become more experienced, begin to say the pitches (C D E F G A B C) while you're playing, as a way of learning where all those notes are in the open position. This skill doesn't come up a lot in my approach to teaching and playing, but if you ever decide to learn to read music, knowing where the notes are on all the strings is an essential skill.

**Example 1f:**

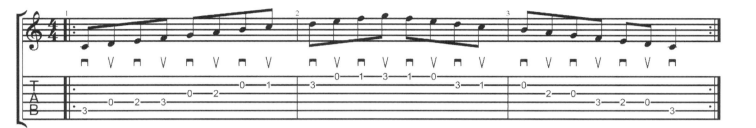

Now onto rhythm.

While I might not place a lot of value on the ability to recognise pitches when reading TAB, developing rhythm skills is *essential*. Being able to read and understand rhythms means you can work from any notation without the need for video or audio to assist. This will add endless confidence to your playing. You'll know exactly where all your notes should fall, and your picking hand will keep you in time.

We'll begin by playing 1/4 notes.

1/4 notes are played on the beats (1 2 3 4), so there are four of them in a bar.

They are all played with downstrokes, but after each pick, you'll bring your hand back up. Even though you're not hitting the strings on the upstroke, the alternating motion should still be there. Remember, the picking hand never stops pumping up and down!

I want you to play this exercise often and, when you do, you HAVE to read it. The point of the exercise is to train rhythm into your brain – not just how to play it, but what it looks like on the page – so that every time you *see* a 1/4 note, you automatically know what it sounds like; and every time you *hear* a 1/4 note, you automatically know how it looks written down.

This process will take time, but it's worth it. It's the same process you used to learn to read words, and reading music is no different when you dedicate yourself to learning that skill.

**Example 1g:**

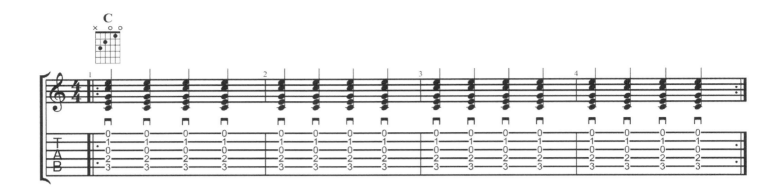

Next up we have 1/8th notes. There will be eight of these to the bar (1 + 2 + 3 + 4 +). Playing them will now require you to hit those upstrokes. You're playing twice as many notes as before, but nothing has changed physically in the picking hand. It shouldn't feel like you're going any faster.

As with the last example, read along with this exercise as you're playing it. Never lose sight of which bar you're on, and which note you're at. We're training the brain here, and it takes time and repetition.

**Example 1h:**

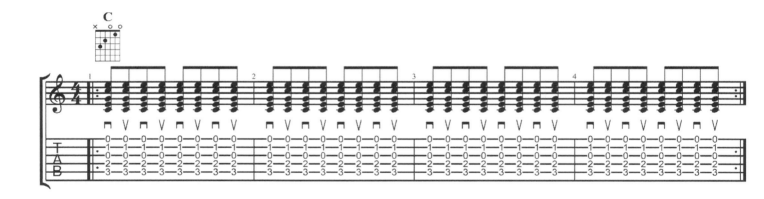

Now we're going to mix 1/4 and 1/8th note rhythms.

Take some time to look at the next example before attempting to play it. Try to imagine what it's going to sound like. You could even vocalise it, if you're confident to do so.

On the audio, I'll count along for the first couple of times through. Listen to how my vocal count lines up with the notes you're playing:

1 2 3 & 4      1 & 2 & 3 4     1 & 2 3 4 &     1 2 & 3 4

Keep a consistent motion in the picking hand at all times.

**Example 1i:**

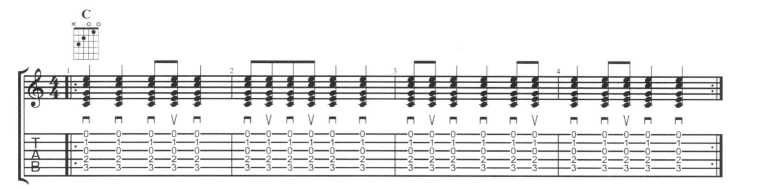

Now you have the rhythm reading idea underway, I want to put a little more pressure on your brain by asking it to process chord changes at the same time. This example features the same rhythm as the previous one, but you need to move between the chords G, D, and C.

Focus on the rhythm and keeping that hand moving!

**Example 1j:**

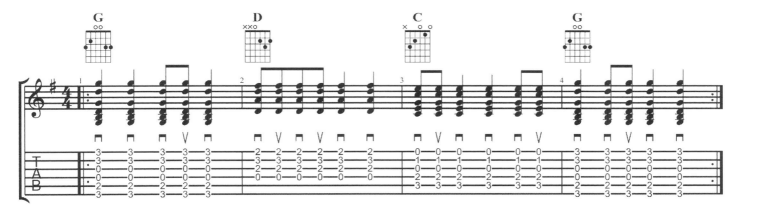

The last few examples have covered strumming technique and next we're going to pick single notes.

Stop and think about that for a moment.

What's the difference in the picking hand between strumming and picking single notes?

The answer is, there doesn't have to be one, and my approach is to blur that line as much as possible.

This example uses the same rhythm again, but this time applied in a single note setting with the C Major scale. There is *slightly more* control required, but the core idea is the same: the picking hand should continue to pump down/up, while picking the rhythm and notes required.

**Example 1k:**

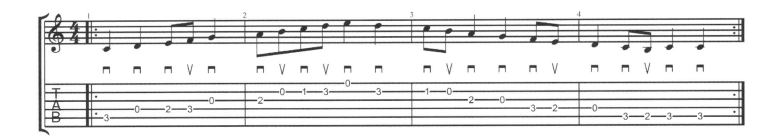

To test that you're starting to understand this, let's apply the concept to a different rhythm and melody. While they are different, the consistent motion of the picking hand is *exactly the same*.

I urge you to look at the page and work out how you think this is going to sound and be played, before you listen to the audio.

Using your ears to copy what you hear is an important skill, and one you're almost certainly already better at than using your eyes, but I want you to be able to see written rhythms and automatically know how they should sound.

**Example 1l:**

The final two examples in the routine are a call-back to examples 1b and 1c. There, you were drilling where all the notes of the C Major scale are on the lowest two strings.

Here we're going to put that to the test, and work on your ability to hear something, process that information, then react to it.

On paper this example looks simple – and it is – but in practice, you may find it a challenge.

In the first bar, I'm going to say a pitch, then you have four beats to find that note on the low E string, ready to play it in bar two.

Then I'll say another note, and you'll have another four beats to find it, ready to play it in the next bar.

On the audio file I'll do this for a fair bit longer than just four bars, so be prepared to be on your toes!

**Example 1m:**

The final example in this routine is the same idea as the last example, now applied to the A string.

This might feel boring, or unrelated, but as you develop your playing through these routines, you'll find that your ability to do things quickly will hinge on your ability to do this effortlessly. You've got to be able to immediately see those root notes!

**Example 1n:**

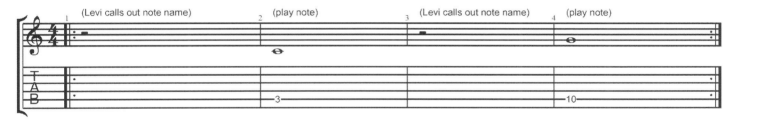

Get to work on this, play along with the routine once a day (more, if you can find the time) and after a week (minimum!) you'll be ready to move on.

Remember the key philosophy of this book:

We don't practice until we can get something *right*, we practice until *we can't get it wrong*.

After a couple of days on this, it will feel like you could move on – and you probably could – but don't!

After 20 years of playing, I can honestly say I've never regretted practicing something, but I have often regretted moving on from something too quickly!

# Routine Two – Rhythm Matters

With routine one out of the way (and at LEAST one week having gone by of you practicing it!) you're back, fresh faced and excited to get onto something new. Thankfully, we have plenty of that here.

Last week you worked on some key skills with an overall emphasis on the alternate motion in your picking hand. This week we're going to build on that and work on playing some syncopated rhythms, while keeping the motion in the picking hand solid.

The picking hand is a weak point for many players. You've probably played a certain way for years, without paying too much attention to it, and now undoing those habits feels like hard work. You may be asking yourself why it matters. Is it that big of a deal? Can't you just press on and make it work for you?

I'd off that the answer is, yes, it's a big deal – and no, you shouldn't just continue with your bad habits. Alternate picking/strumming is the most efficient way to play. You should be able to do this and if you look at it in the cold light of day, I think you'll agree it's silly not to be able to do something so simple. Please don't feel bad about needing to work on it, because you can do this! You just need to persevere.

When it clicks into place, suddenly it will feel completely effortless to you, and you'll wonder why you never corrected this aspect of your technique before. Mastering your instrument and achieving your goals isn't supposed to be easy – nothing worth doing is. But every day you're getting better, so keep at it!

Here are the learning objectives for this routine:

- Develop further dexterity in the fretting hand

- Learn moving pentatonic scales

- Execute syncopated rhythms

- Practice the motion of the picking hand

- Identify sharp and flat notes on the E and A strings


Let's get to work!

First up, we're going to revisit an idea from the previous routine. This time, instead of using a 1234 fingering pattern, we'll switch it up to 1324.

Remember the approach from last week: *finger goes down, pick hits string.*

This principle becomes more important now. When playing the note with the middle finger, you're not lifting the ring finger up to reveal a pre-fretted note, the middle finger goes down as the pick hits the string.

**Example 2a:**

Over the coming routines we're going to be working on a lot of barre forms – i.e. shapes on the fretboard that can be played as both chords/arpeggios and scales. The end goal is that you are to play any chord, arpeggio or scale in any key. To reach that goal, however, you need to build some confidence with the concept.

In Example 2b, you'll play the E Minor Pentatonic scale from routine one, then move the whole shape up one fret. The root note of the scale is now on the E string, 1st fret, rather than the open low E. We've moved from E Minor Pentatonic to F Minor Pentatonic. Keep that picking hand moving down-up continually.

**Example 2b:**

Now we're going to apply this movable shape to some different keys: C Minor, F Minor, G Minor, D Minor and A Minor. The pattern is exactly the same as Example 2b, so focus on moving the root note up/down the neck to locate the scale shape in the right place. C Minor Pentatonic has the root note on the low E string, 8th fret; G Minor Pentatonic is at the 3rd fret, and so on.

One of the most important skills you're developing here is to *look ahead*. Your ultimate goal is to be able to play the scale shape so that your mind is free to forget about what you're playing. That will take care of itself, while you begin to think about where you need to move next.

This is the most basic multitasking skill we need to master on the guitar. It will feel impossible at first, but before long you'll automatically look into the future all the time.

**Example 2c:**

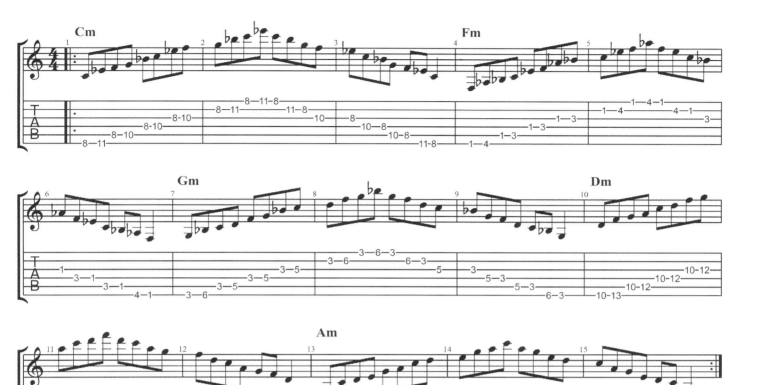

Now it's time to move on to a series of exercises that deal with syncopated rhythms. Before we get into them, I want you to play the rhythm in Example 2d. Try it without listening to the audio to begin with. Remember, this should be something you can decipher with your eyes, not copy with your ears. It's just a simple application of 1/8th and 1/4 notes.

**Example 2d:**

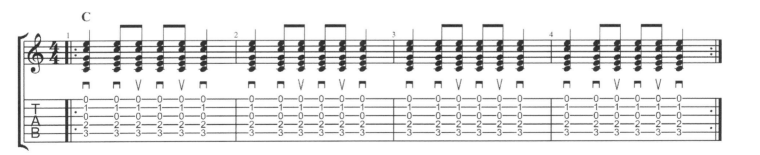

The next example is almost identical, but this time skips playing the first 1/8th note on beat 2. This could be considered a *syncopation*. Syncopation is a musical device which involves shifting the place where the strong accents are perceived in the music. So, rather than placing a strong, equal emphasis on beats 1, 2, 3 and 4, here we're pushing the emphasis on beat 2 to the "2&".

From a technical perspective, the trick to playing this smoothly is to keep your picking hand moving continuously, not just hitting that second downstroke. You're probably well used to *not* hitting the strings when the pick comes back up from a downstroke, so this should be relatively easy.

If you read the rhythmic notation, you'll notice that bars 3-4 look different from bars 1-2. In the first two bars, I've notated the rhythm with a tie between the first 1/4 note and 1/8th note. In the second two bars, I used a dotted 1/4 note. They sound the same but the latter is the more common way of writing the rhythm.

A dot after a note adds half the length again to the note. In other words, a dotted 1/4 note lasts 50% longer than a regular 1/4 note. That sounds a whole lot like maths, right? It is, but it doesn't need to be. Treat it like language. Work on this exercise for a long time and read it while you're doing it. Train your mind to *see* these rhythms and to know what they'll sound like.

**Example 2e:**

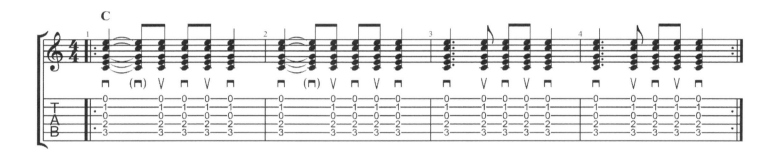

Here's that same rhythm, now applied to some chord changes: G major, D major, C major, G major.

**Example 2f:**

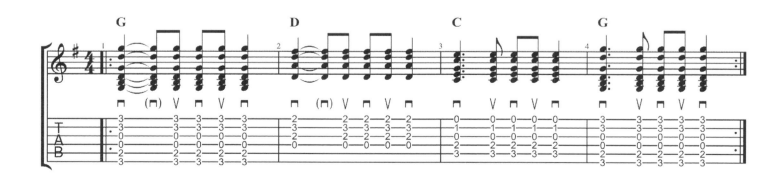

The previous example didn't contain enough of an emphasis on the chord to be a syncopation (in my mind, at least). It was more that you just didn't play a note. In the next example, however, you're going to play *down-up*, skip the next *down*, then an *up*.

As with many rhythms, this is easy to hear and copy. It's harder to process it visually, and understand it just with your mind, but it will benefit you to do so.

Again, I've notated this two ways. They sound the same, but the second is the more common to see.

**Example 2g:**

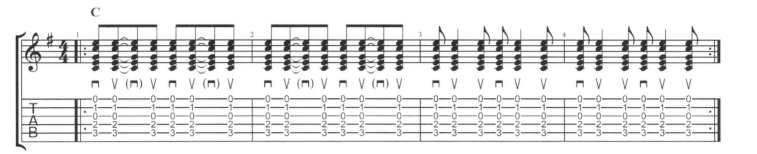

Here's a classic syncopated rhythm that has a tie into beat 3. You'll only see this type of rhythm written one way, as it's considered poor etiquette to have a 1/4 note that goes through the middle of the bar.

**Example 2h:**

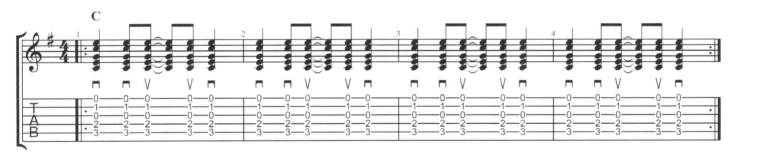

With these rhythms under your fingers, let's mix them up and apply them to some chord changes. To give you a little more of a challenge, I've removed the picking directions. You have to know the basic rhythms to play this!

**Example 2i:**

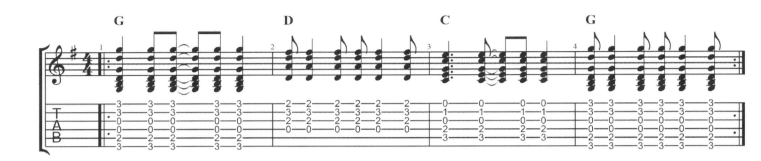

So far, you've applied these rhythms to chords. Now we're going to refine the picking hand motion down to a single note. Note that the motion of your picking hand is *not* changing – you'll still swing it up and down – you're just focusing the motion onto a single string.

Also…

Read it. Every. Time.

**Example 2j:**

With this exercise under your belt, next you'll apply the exact same rhythm to a different single note idea to play more of a melody. Even though you'll now need to move between strings, the motion in the picking hand is the same. Keep the hand moving up and down at all times and pick the strings when you need them to sound.

**Example 2k:**

We're going to finish this week with more of a mental exercise.

Last week we located the notes of the C Major scale (C D E F G A B) on the E and A strings. This week we're going to add sharps and flats into the equation.

Flat (b) notes will always be one fret below a named note. So, to find Bb for example, go to B (7th fret) and move down one fret to Bb. Db will be at the 9th fret, one fret below D, etc.

Sharp (#) notes will be one fret higher than a named note. F# will be at the 2nd fret, one fret above F. D# will be at the 11th fret, one fret above D, etc.

In the early stages, it's fine to treat locating flat/sharp notes as a two-step process. You will locate the regular note, then make it flat or sharp. As you continue to do this, however, in time you'll just know where the note is. Trust the process!

Let's start on the E string.

**Example 2l:**

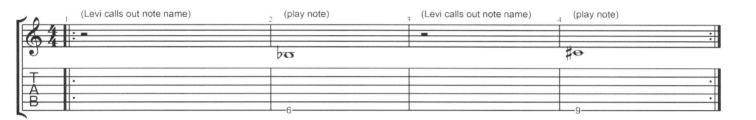

Now finish up on the A string.

**Example 2m:**

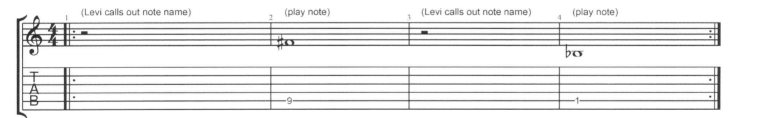

That's another week down. Get to work and I'll catch you when you're ready to move on!

# Routine Three – Picking Drills

One of the challenges of writing practice routines is that it's hard to find a balance between everything you need to work on and keeping the session interesting (without it taking 90 minutes to complete!)

In last week's routine, we focused on visualising and understanding rhythms, but didn't do any heavy technical drills or discuss any theory. I'd love to include all of those elements in every routine, but if I did, you'd only have one exercise per idea, and that doesn't work! So, this week I'm guiding you through some more challenging picking ideas and we'll work on expanding your chord knowledge.

Our learning objectives this week are:

- Increasing fretting hand dexterity

- Triplets versus 1/8th notes

- Cross-picking skills

- Minor chords

There's an element of bluegrass influence in this routine. While I'm not a bluegrass player myself, I've always been in awe of great pickers like Tony Rice and David Grier. These are guys who have spent a lifetime picking their guitars, and there's not even a hint of "inconvenience" in their playing. Whereas a rock player might organise their licks to suit their technique, or a straight-ahead blues player might avoid playing more technically challenging ideas, a bluegrass player will just pick it!

It can't be easy to do this, but I respect the ethos of these players immensely. Wouldn't you like to be able to just pick any piece of music you were required to? Me too! So, let's do some work on that skill. Once again, we'll start the routine with a basic chromatic warm-up, but this time you'll play with a 1423 configuration. As always, remember our mantra: *finger goes down, pick hits string.*

**Example 3a:**

I mentioned at the beginning of routine one that, though they have their uses, I'm not crazy about chromatic warm-ups. I see much more value in picking through a scale shape, which doesn't force your picking hand into a repetitive, string-crossing mechanic. Plus, these chromatic patterns are not the kind of thing we play when soloing, whereas scalar shapes are. So, next we play an open position C Major scale, ascending and descending. Keep that picking hand moving down and up!

**Example 3b:**

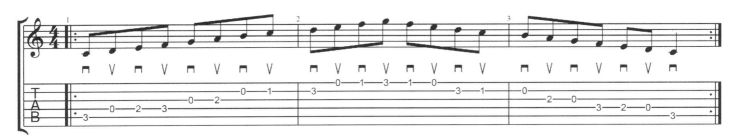

Next, we move on to look at triplet rhythms. The previous exercise was played using straight 1/8th notes. We could say there are eight of them in a bar, but another way to look at them is that there are two notes per beat in a bar of 4/4.

This is a good frame of reference to help us understand that 1/8th note triplets occur when we play *three* notes in each beat.

We count straight 1/8th notes, 1-&, 2-&, 3-&, 4-&

But we count 1/8th note triplets, 1-&-a, 2-&-a, 3-&-a, 4-&-a

Notice in the notation that triplets look like three 1/8th notes grouped together, and they have a bracket over them with a number 3, indicating that they are triplets.

Exercise 3c alternates between bars of 1/8th notes and 1/8th note triplets. In order to execute this, your picking hand needs to accelerate when you shift into the triplets. Repetition is the key to this skill, but it shouldn't take long to get down.

**Example 3c:**

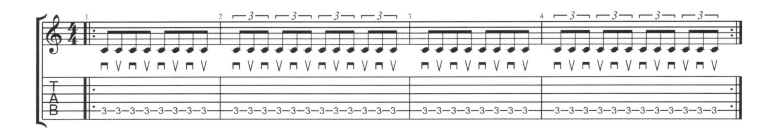

Now you have a feel for how triplets sound, let's apply the rhythm to the open position C Major scale. You might expect this to be similar to playing straight 1/8th notes, but in fact the feel is completely different, so take your time.

**Example 3d:**

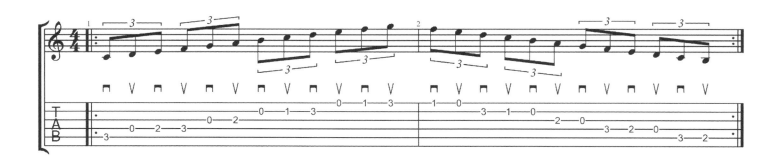

To make things a little more challenging, let's mix 1/8th notes and 1/8th note triplets playing the C Major scale. Here, you'll play two beats of 1/8th notes (four notes) followed by two beats of triplets (six notes). There's a lot of control required here, as your picking hand has to change gear every two beats. Make sure you can count it before you play it!

**Example 3e:**

Next we're going to apply alternate picking to some repeating arpeggio sequences that contain triplets. Variation in music is what keeps things interesting. Running up and down scales can get boring fast, so being fluent with arpeggios can only add more interest to your playing.

The problem with arpeggio application on guitar is that picking across multiple strings is technically demanding. Picking one note on each string is often called "cross picking", though the name doesn't come from how cross you are after having to practice it.

In this example, you'll first pick though a C major chord in 1/8th notes, then repeat it on just the A, D and G strings, with alternate picked 1/8th note triplets.

This might feel easy when done slowly, but as the speed picks up you'll feel like the strings are trying to trip you up all the time. It requires dedication.

**Example 3f:**

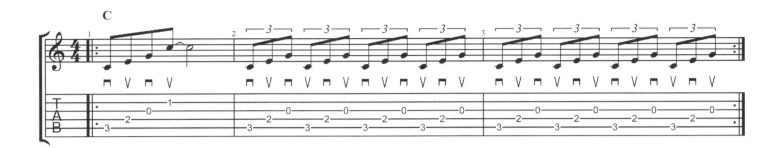

Now we're going to take the picking pattern from the previous example and apply it to some chord changes. These types of exercises are great fun because they allow us to keep working on a technique in the picking hand but force us to do it in a more subconscious way, because we have to give some attention to the fretting hand.

**Example 3g:**

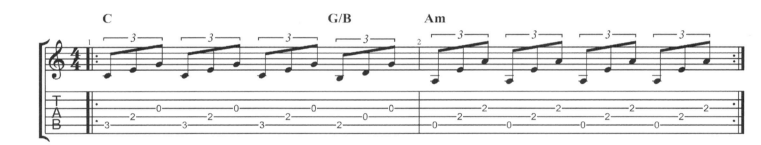

If you've been paying attention to the chord symbols in the notation so far, you might point out that we've not played any minor chords yet, so let's address that now.

Let's remind ourselves what a minor chord is. A major chord is formed from the root, 3rd and 5th of the major scale, but a minor chord contains the root, b3 and 5th. In other words, a minor chord is a major chord but with the 3rd lowered a half step.

Here are the E, A and D open major chords, each followed by their minor equivalent. Notice that I've left out the C and G shapes. While these can be played, the reality is that the corresponding minor shapes are extremely awkward to use and are never played in open or barred positions.

**Example 3h:**

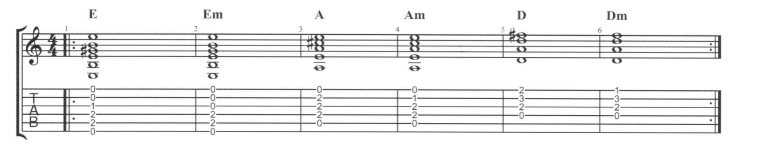

Now let's combine some major and minor chords to make a longer chord progression. I wanted to make it a little more challenging at the end, where you'll play 1/4 and 1/8th notes. These movements might take time to get under your fingers, but that's natural.

**Example 3i:**

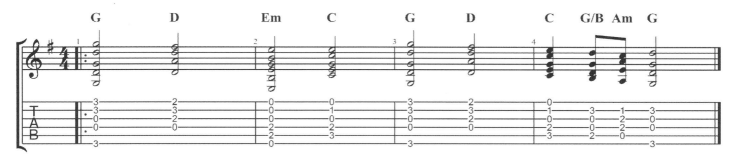

Once you're familiar with a chord progression like this, you can apply picking patterns to make the progression sound more musical. Here I'm applying triplets. This is more demanding for the picking hand, so take this slow at first.

**Example 3j:**

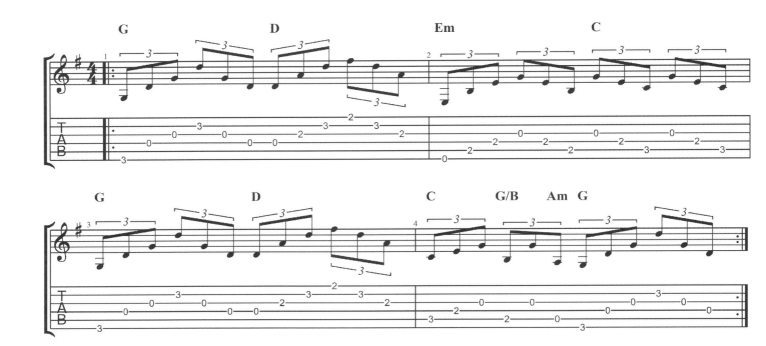

The final example is a little longer and uses all three of the minor chords. Mixing up chords like this, applying different picking patterns, will put your picking hand through its paces, but is well worth the time. I've been playing guitar for 20 years and I wish I'd done this more when I was a teen!

**Example 3k:**

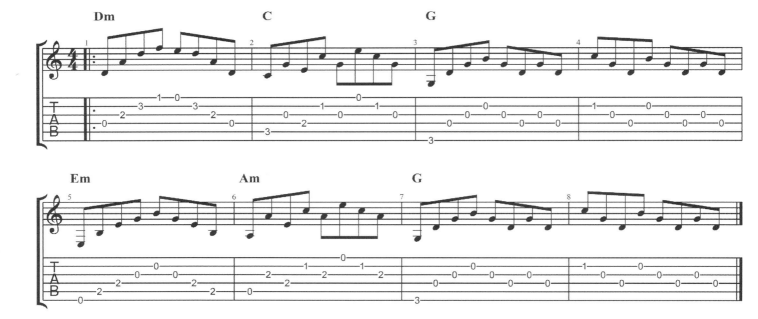

# Routine Four – Barre Chords

After spending a solid week working on alternate picking skills, single note fingering dexterity and scale patterns, we're going to switch up our goals and spend some time looking at barre chords using the E and A shapes. We'll apply strumming patterns to these shapes with progressions that move up and down the neck.

Whether you're new to barre chords or you've been playing them for a long time, I'm sure you can recall the jump in difficulty from playing open chords. There is much more fretting hand strength required to barre all six strings with consistent pressure, even for minutes, let alone hours at a time.

First, a tip about barring. The thumb will be placed on the back of the neck, while the index finger holds the barre on the fretboard. Think of it as a pinching movement, but make sure you're not applying too much pressure – you're not trying to break the neck here, and you can use a lot less force than you think!

I don't want to scare anyone, but physical injuries can sneak up on you when you play lots of guitar. Don't put too much stress on your body for prolonged periods of time. Go easy on yourself!

Our learning objectives today are:

• E shape major barre chords

• E shape minor barre chords

• Johann Pachelbel's *Canon in D* chord progression

• A shape major barre chords

• A shape minor barre chords

• Syncopated strumming patterns


Although we are working on chords this week, we'll warm up by playing the open position C Major scale to get the fretting hand fingers moving. By the end of this book, I'll have said this 100 times, but I can't overstress it's importance: keep that picking hand moving!

**Example 4a:**

We'll begin with a reminder of where a barre chord comes from, by playing an open E major chord, fingered as normal with the index, middle and ring fingers. Play the open E then move everything up one fret. Use the index finger to barre across all six strings, then place the middle, ring, and pinky finger to fret the remaining notes of the chord.

Next, move up from F to F#, then from F# to G, and back down again.

Note that you don't need to maintain your barre pressure when shifting up or down the neck. But at the same time, you don't want to lift your fingers away from the strings. The trick is to release just enough pressure, so that shifting the hand along the neck feels effortless.

**Example 4b:**

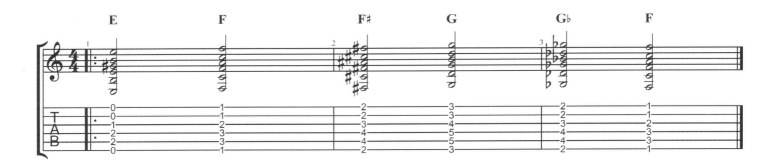

Now repeat this exercise with minor chords. This should feel slightly easier as you're using one less finger, but keep your focus on the pressure and control.

**Example 4c:**

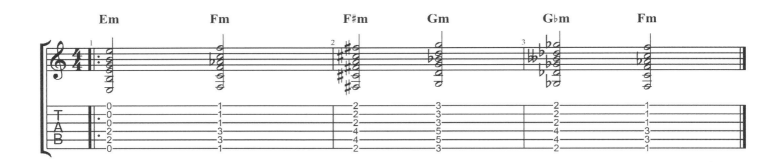

Now we're going to apply the major and minor voicings in a chord progression. This sequence comes from Johann Pachelbel's *Canon in D*. First of all, familiarise yourself with the progression:

D major – A major – B minor – F# minor – G major – D major – G major – A major

When you've committed this to memory, play the example below, moving your barre chord shapes to the correct root note on the E string. D major is located at the 10th fret, A major is at the 5th, B minor is at the 7th, etc.

**Example 4d:**

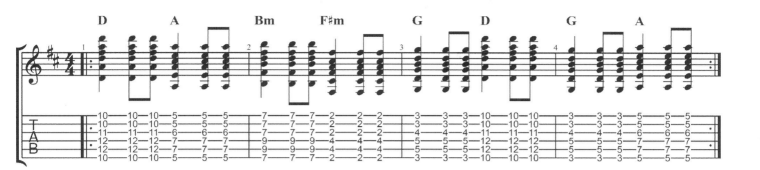

Now let's repeat the process with the open A chord.

When playing an open A chord, it's common to keep the high E string in this chord. This can be included in the barre form too, but not without some complications, so for now we'll omit it. When you move into the barre forms, use your index finger to play the root note on the A string, then the ring or pinky finger to barre the remaining three notes.

**Example 4e:**

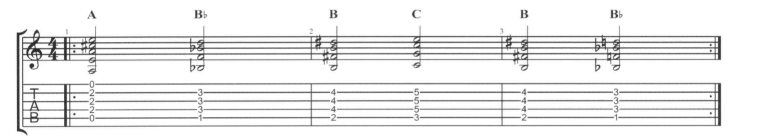

It's much easier to include the high E string note in A minor shape barre chords and get it to ring cleanly.

**Example 4f:**

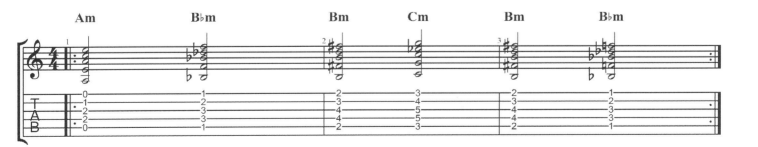

Now you're familiar with the A shape, we're going to apply it to Pachelbel's *Canon in D*. The chord sequence is the same but now the root notes are in different locations. D major is at the 5th fret on the A string, A major is an open chord, B minor is at the 2nd fret, and so on.

**Example 4g:**

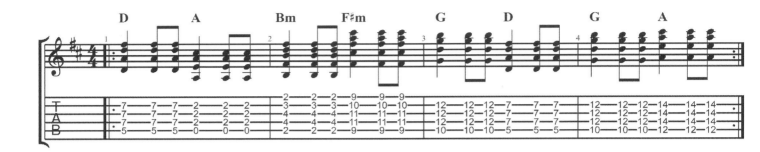

It would be fair to say that the two pathways we used to play through this progression were harder than they needed to be, because we limited ourselves to using one option each time. The jump from B minor using the A shape, to F# minor in the A shape is seven frets, for instance. That's more demanding on the player but also more work for the listener, as the chords feel less related.

The solution, of course, is to combine E and A shapes to create a more economical pathway. There's no reason, for example, to play D major at the 5th fret, then jump all the way down to the open position for A major when you can stay at the 5th fret and just move over to the low E string.

Here's an alternative way to play through the progression.

**Example 4h:**

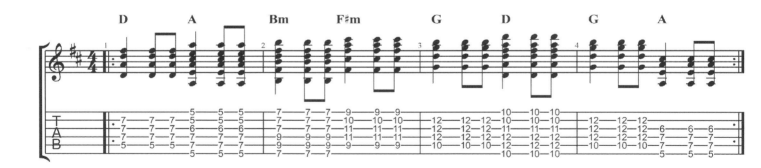

The skill here is to find the nearest root note on the E and A strings. You worked on this in the first two routines, but you can always be better at it!

Here's another way through the same chord progression.

**Example 4i:**

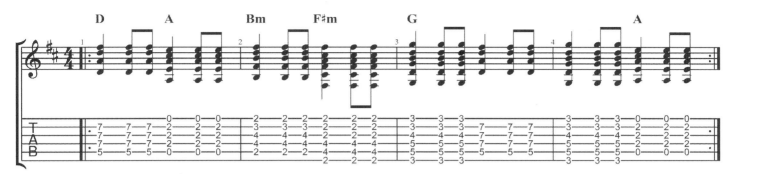

Next, we're going to delve a little deeper into the syncopated rhythms we began to look at earlier. In the next exercise you'll play a downstroke on beat 1, skip beat 2, then play an upstroke on the "&" of beat 2.

It's played with a straight feel here. If you move into the world of swing, this rhythm is referred to as the Charleston, named after the popular 1920's dance.

**Example 4j:**

With this rhythm under your belt, we'll apply it to a chord progression that combines major and minor chords with E and A string roots.

**Example 4k:**

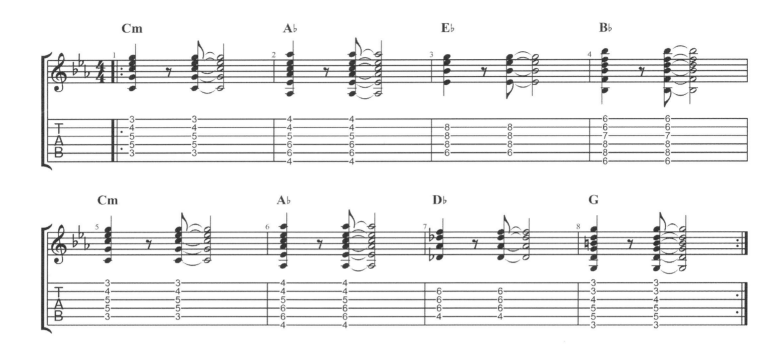

Now we're going to work on the trickiest syncopated rhythm yet. It's one that appears to "float" over the bar. Take this one real slow at first. To create the floating effect, you'll play an upstroke on the "&" of beat 4 and hold it over into the next bar, without hitting the downstroke. Then you'll play on beat 2.

The fretting hand should keep moving throughout this – you're just not striking the strings on the down beat of bar two. It sounds like it should be very easy, but it's consistently a point of great struggle for students, so it's worth drilling. Don't give up, you'll get it.

**Example 4l:**

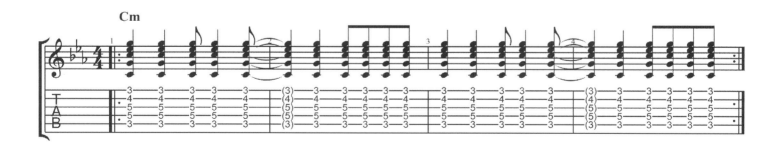

Our final example for this week takes the previous rhythm and applies it to the progression from Example 4j. This requires you to give some attention to the fretting hand, so that hopefully the picking hand will begin to move subconsciously.

**Example 4m:**

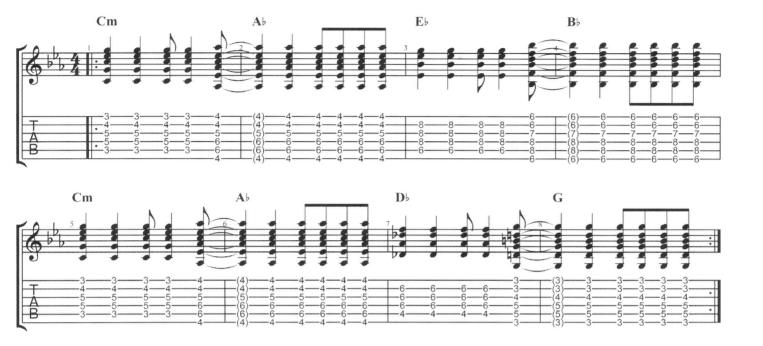

Keep it up, and I'll see you in a week!

# Routine Five – E Shape Major Scale

Now you've put some time into barre chords, it's time to take that knowledge of movable shapes and return to focusing on picking hand technique by looking at movable major scales.

The C Major scale in the open position we're now familiar with is great for a warm-up, but doesn't help if we want to play a D Major scale. For that, we need a moveable shape that can serve us in any situation.

When it comes to applying scales, one of the biggest problems I've seen with students is that they only ever play them "as scales" i.e. they play them up and down, beginning on the root note. Then, they struggle to stop them sounding like scales when they want to make music.

I want to try and break that habit immediately by moving you towards being able to play from any point in a scale. If you can develop that skill, you'll be able to transition to wherever you want to go without having to jump down to a low root note.

After that, we'll look at some sequencing ideas that will help you break the habit of running up and down scales – all the while increasing your fretting hand dexterity.

The learning objectives this week include:

- C shape barre chords

- E shape major scale

- Top, middle and bottom scale starting points

- "4s" sequences

You'll notice I've included another barre chord shape here. That's because I want you to have more options at your disposal than the two covered thus far. In the long run, you'll come to understand that chords are quick visual references that serve as "snapshots" for you to play scales around. The more chords you know, the more melodic ideas you'll be able to play.

We're going to start like last week, with a major scale ascending and descending, but this time we're playing it as triplets. Being able to subdivide the beat as you choose is one of the ultimate tests of control. Once again, keep that picking hand moving!

**Example 5a:**

Now we need to look at the C shape barre chord. This is, without doubt, the most overlooked chord on the guitar, yet it's also one of the best.

Play the open C chord, fretting it as normal, then move everything up one fret. This requires a change of fingering. The pinky frets the A string root note, the ring finger takes care of the D string, the index finger the G string, and the middle finger frets the B string.

Don't worry about trying to barre across all five strings with the index finger for this shape – just assign it to fretting the note on the G string. I'd also encourage you to place your thumb higher up the neck, rather than in the middle, to relieve pressure on the fretting hand.

Again, we're omitting the high E string note in the barre chords, but if you want to include it you can do so by flattening the index finger to barre the top three strings.

Play C major, then move up to C# major, D major, E major, then back down again. Remember to release most of the pressure as you move between chords. There's no reason to squeeze and make your life harder.

**Example 5b:**

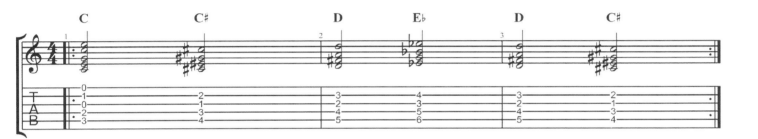

Now we're going to include this new barre chord shape in a progression, to get it under your fingers quickly. The struggle with any new chord is to form it quickly enough to keep playing the progression smoothly. That's where most people fall down with the C shape. They learn it, find it tricky, then label it as something to avoid. Not here, though. Let's master it!

The chord progression is C minor – Ab major – Eb major – G major. You'll play shapes you already know except in bar three, where the C shape barre is introduced.

For extra practice, see where you can include the C shape barre chord in progressions you already know.

**Example 5c:**

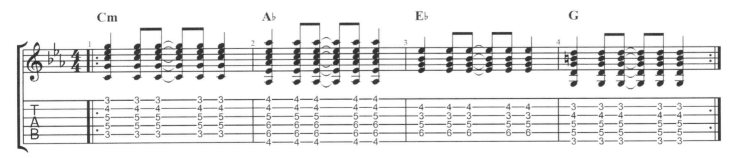

Now we move on to drilling the major scale pattern, played around the E shape barre chord form.

When doing this, I always recommend playing the chord first, then the scale. It's a good way of helping the brain to build an association between the chord and the scale. As you play through the scale, you're hitting the notes contained in the chord, and it helps you to understand how they're interlinked.

As with all previous examples, keep that picking hand moving. It's about consistent motion, but also consistent dynamics.

**Example 5d:**

Now we're going to play the same thing but in the key of D Major. Move the chord up to the 10th fret and the pattern follows.

This is where the guitar shines – it's a shape-based instrument and we can use that to our advantage. I also play the piano and I can assure you, learning scales in 12 keys is a lot of work. Every scale has a different combination of black and white keys, and the fingerings vary from key to key and hand to hand. It's a LOT to remember. By comparison, the guitar is easy, so use its benefits to your advantage.

**Example 5e:**

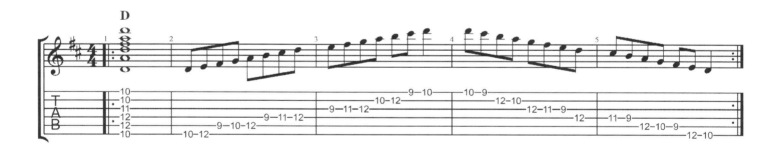

As mentioned in the introduction to this routine, it's important to practice and know scales from locations other than the root note. If a student is soloing and I suggest using a different scale, it's common to see them jump down to its low root note to access it. This is the opposite of the freedom you want knowledge to provide you with.

So, in this exercise, you'll play the major scale again, but this time from the root note on the high E string.

To keep things interesting, you'll play it as both straight 1/8th notes then 1/8th note triplets.

**Example 5f:**

Now repeat the exercise in the key of C Major. Play the C major chord, then descend the scale in 1/8th notes and 1/8th note triplets.

**Example 5g:**

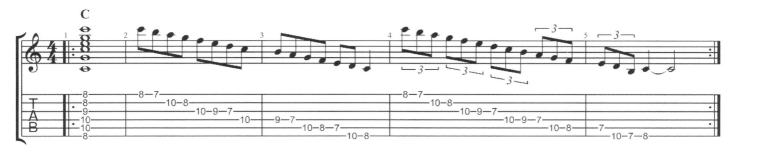

You've played the major scale from the bottom and the top, so this time we'll increase the challenge and play it from the root note in the middle of the scale. While this sounds as easy as the other two, it probably won't be, but we can fix that.

**Example 5h:**

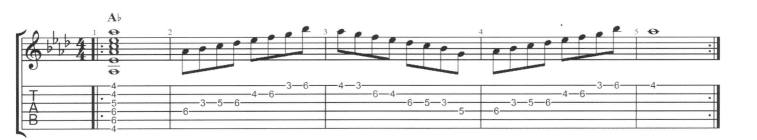

Let's repeat the exercise in the key of Eb up at the 11th fret. Your goal is to be confident doing this in any key. If someone calls out a random key, you should instantly be able to jump to the right location on the neck and play the notes.

**Example 5i:**

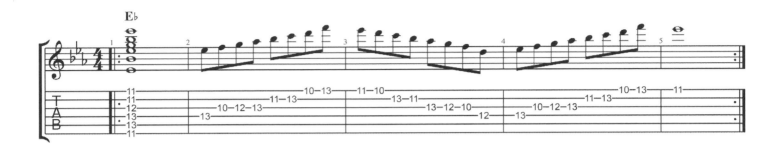

So far, we've played the scales in a linear way, so now we'll move on to some sequences. In this context, a "sequence" can be thought of as a musical pattern. Patterns in music are great because they're something a listener can immediately latch onto, while making the music sound more interesting than just playing a scale.

The first sequence we're going to look at can be thought of as *ascending fours*. If we assign each note of the scale a number from one to eight, then starting from the first note, ascending fours would follow this pattern:

1234 – 2345 – 3456 – 4567 – 5678 etc

In other words, we ascend four notes from the root, then go back to the second note in the scale and ascend four notes from there, then return to the third note, etc.

Here's that pattern played in the first octave of the scale.

**Example 5j:**

Now, here's the same sequence, this time played in the second octave of the E shape major scale.

**Example 5k:**

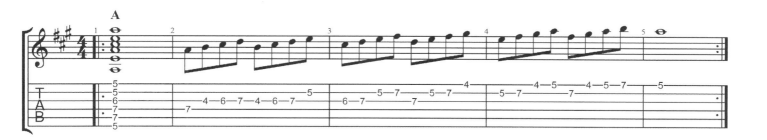

We can combine both of octaves to make one longer exercise.

Once you're comfortable with this pattern, move it around and play it in different keys until you can do so without thinking about it. Keep that hand moving!

**Example 5l:**

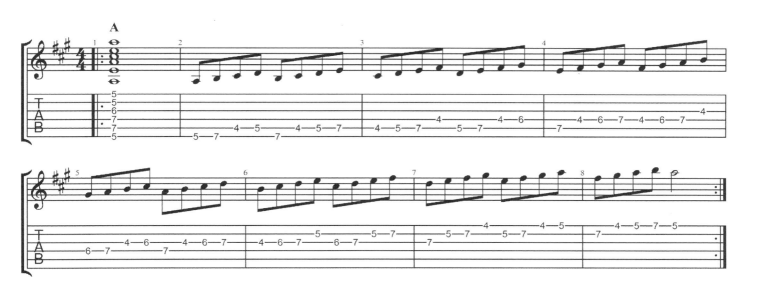

Finally, here's the descending version of that sequence played over two octaves:

8765 – 7654 – 6543 – 5432 – 4321 etc

**Example 5m:**

Good luck, and I'll see you in a week!

# Routine Six – Strumming & Pentatonics

Hopefully you didn't find last week too taxing. There was a lot to remember with no new technical challenges being presented. We're going to flip that this week and focus on some of the more technical aspects of playing. We'll even delve into some more musical ideas at the end.

One way you could look at the majority of the material in this book is that we are programming in our alternate picking motion. First, we did that with strumming ideas, then refined the motion down to single note ideas. It's all the same motion, we're just dealing with levels of control.

Today we're going to blend those two elements together by introducing single notes into our strumming patterns. This will give us more folk and country sounding chordal patterns with alternating bass notes.

We'll also start looking at major pentatonic sounds, which you can think of as stripped back versions of the major scale. You'll find that a lot of popular music relies more on the pentatonic scale than the full major scale, as it occupies a nice middle ground between a chord (three notes) and a full scale (seven notes).

Our learning objectives today are:

• Outside picking technique

• Alternating bass note strumming patterns

• Bass note walk down

• Major pentatonic scale

• Bluegrass melody


Let's begin with a warm-up.

This week we're going back to the 1234 style warm-up, but we'll mix it up a little by introducing some string crossing.

This time you'll play 1 on the E string, 2 on the A string, 3 on the E string and 4 on the A string. This will demand a bit more concentration.

As you pick through it, you'll find you're playing a downstroke on the E string and an upstroke on the A string, and your pick stays on the outside of these two strings. We call this *outside picking*.

You can try *inside picking* by playing an upstroke on the E and a downstroke on the A. Many players find this motion harder, but in the long run we want to get good at both approaches, rather than avoiding one.

**Example 6a:**

With the warm-up done, we're going to move on to some strumming patterns that include alternating bass notes. To begin, let's try this with a C major chord.

Start by fretting the open C chord as normal. First, play the bass note on the A string, then strum the top four strings down and up. Then, move your ring finger over to the E string, play the lower bass note, then strum the top four strings again twice.

The first bass note falls on beat 1 and the second bass note falls on beat 3.

Play it slowly to begin with the get the movement down. This pattern/movement needs to become automatic to you, so stick with it.

**Example 6b:**

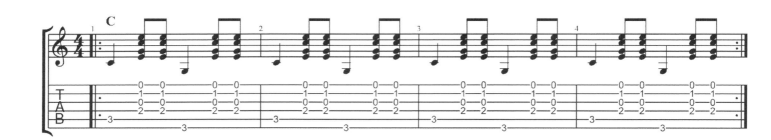

If we play the same idea using an open E chord, we can't play a bass note lower than the first one, so we need a different note. The solution is to alternate with a note on the A string.

In both examples, we're alternating between the root note and 5th of the chord, which is a common bass pattern in this style.

**Example 6c:**

When playing the same idea on a D major chord, you'll alternate between the D string bass note on beat 1 and the A string on beat 3. As before, these are the root and 5th of the D chord.

I always find the D shape a little trickier than the other two patterns, mainly because I don't tend to see the root notes on the D string as easily, as it's so high in pitch.

**Example 6d:**

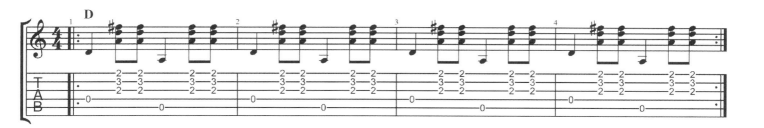

Now let's apply these patterns to a chord progression, so you get a feel for moving alternating bass note patterns between string sets. Don't be put off by the first chord not being a C, it still has its root note on the A string, so you're still alternating between the A and E strings for the bass notes.

**Example 6e:**

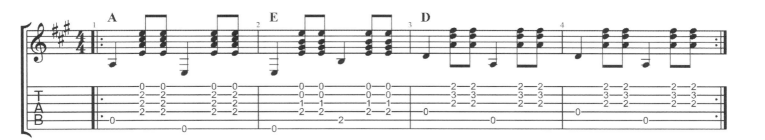

The idea behind this style of strumming is to create the effect of two independent instruments – a guitar playing the chords and a bass playing the bass notes. We can take this idea to the next level by making the bass parts more interesting.

In this example we'll add a bass note walkdown from the C chord in bar one to the A minor chord in bar two.

**Example 6f:**

Here's a longer idea that uses more minor chords for a darker sound. The technique is still the same – you need to control the alternating bass motion as the chords move between different string sets.

**Example 6g:**

Now we turn our attention to the major pentatonic scale. As mentioned in the introduction, the pentatonic is the middle ground between the major triad and the seven-note major scale.

A major triad contains the root, 3rd and 5th degrees of the major scale. The major pentatonic scale is that triad, plus the 2nd and 6th degrees. It's commonly used in blues, country, bluegrass, rock, and many more styles of music. You should know it well – both how to play it and how it sounds.

Play through it ascending and descending.

**Example 6h:**

Now, let's add some rhythm to the pattern by moving between 1/4 and 1/8th notes as we play through the scale. Keep the picking hand moving, down, down up.

**Example 6i:**

One of the quickest ways to make this scale sound more musical is to add in the b3 (from the minor chord) as an approach note to the 3rd. It sounds good and is something you should bake into your playing as fast as possible.

In order to execute this example, I play the 5th fret on the G string with my middle finger, then shift the same finger up a fret to the 6th, rather than using two fingers.

**Example 6j:**

The final example in this routine is a little longer. It outlines the melody from a fiddle standard called *Arkansas Traveller*.

Such tunes are often played incredibly fast on the bluegrass scene, so take your time and build up speed over time.

Notice that the melody is played using almost entirely the notes of D Major Pentatonic. The only exception is the 9th fret on the high E string, used in bar seven.

**Example 6k:**

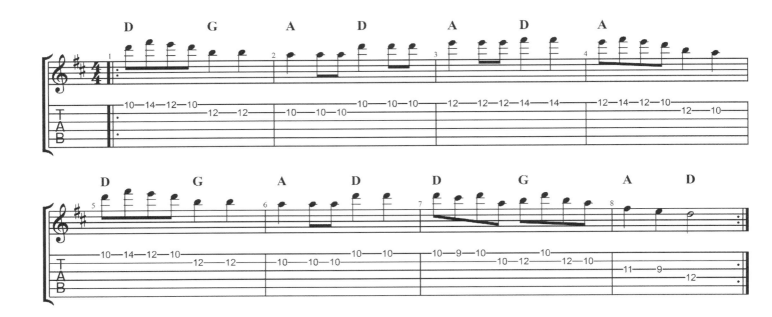

Here's the second section to the tune. You're higher up the neck here, in unfamiliar territory, so take your time.

**Example 6l:**

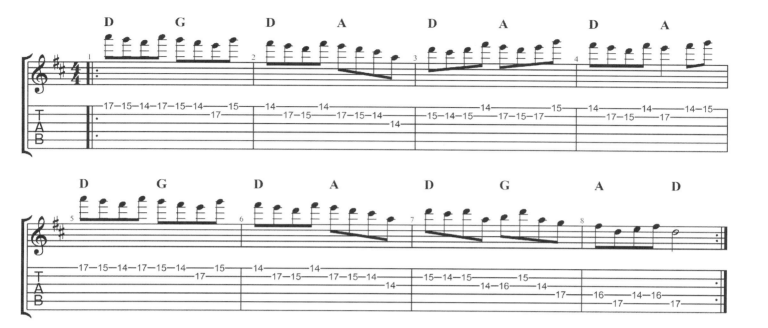

See you next week!

# Routine Seven – C Shape Major Scale

As you might have guessed, we're using three primary chord shapes throughout these routines, so it follows that we're going to master three scale shapes around those chords. Two weeks ago you drilled the E shape major scale pattern, now it's the turn of the C shape.

We're also going to introduce the idea of the Circle of 5ths/4ths in this lesson. This concept is going to come up more and more as we practice, because it's a useful tool to help us practice exercises in different positions in all 12 keys.

You'll see images of the Circle of 5ths all over the internet, but I'm going to present it in a more linear way.

If you start on the note C, then move up seven frets (an interval of a 5th), you arrive at G. If you repeat the exercise from G, you arrive at D, then A, and so on. Do this twelve times and you get the following sequence of notes:

C – G – D – A – E – B – F# – Db – Ab – Eb – Bb – F – C

You end up back where you started.

If you do the same with 4th intervals (take a note, then ascend five frets this time), you get the following sequence:

C – F – Bb – Eb – Ab – Db – F# – B – E – A – D – G – C

You can see that this is the exact same sequence of notes, but backwards. This is known as the Circle of 4ths.

The Circle of 4ths is really useful because it's considered a strong movement, where each chord resolves nicely to the next. It's a much more musical way of moving an idea through all the keys, rather than moving up a semitone at a time.

Here are our learning objectives today:

• Learn the Circle of 4ths

• Drill the C shape major scale

• Learn a scale sequence in 3rds

• Combine arpeggios and scales


Let's get on with the routine then!

We'll start by playing our three major chord shapes using the Circle of 4ths movement. The first chord is C major using the C shape, followed by F major using the E shape, then Bb using the A shape, and so on. It's a great drill for testing your knowledge of the barre shapes and to help embed them in your playing. This may feel hard at first, but take your time and you'll have it committed to memory in no time.

**Example 7a:**

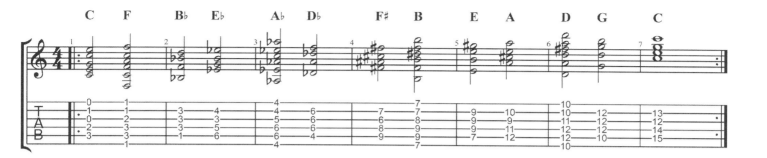

After that chordal workout, we return to the major scale, using the C shape. You've already played this a number of times in the open position. You'll repeat that pattern, then move a semitone higher to play a Db major chord followed by the Db Major scale. Then you'll move another half step up to do the same again with D major.

This is an overlooked scale shape, but it's useful, so get it in there.

**Example 7b:**

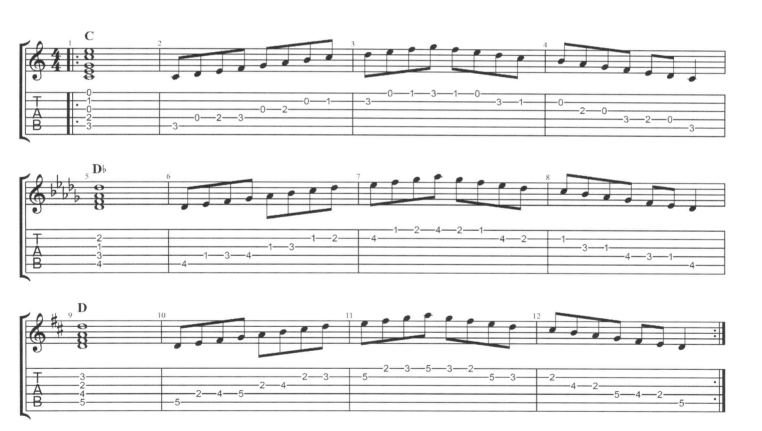

Let's move the same scale pattern higher up the neck and play it from the top down in the key of G. Notice that I've skipped a note at the end so we can finish on the G root note.

**Example 7c:**

The next example moves the scale pattern down to an E major chord and plays the scale from the bottom up, but there's a twist here in the final bar. Here, we're going to descend the triad arpeggio rather than the scale.

**Example 7d:**

Now we'll apply the ascending 4s sequence we touched on two weeks ago. This is the first step in breaking out of scale patterns. Eventually, it will become second nature to play this fingering, rather than being something you have to practice before you can play it.

**Example 7e:**

Remember, it's also important to practice this sequence descending too! When you're comfortable with this, try it in a few different keys.

**Example 7f:**

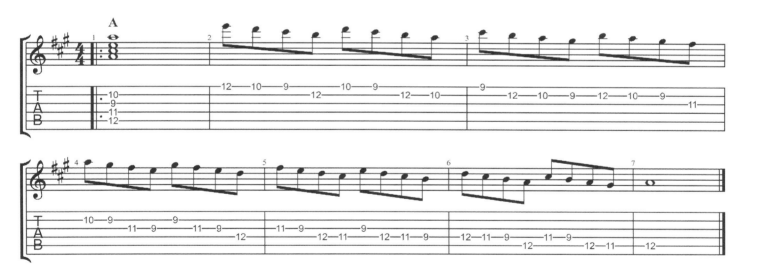

Now it's time to play a new sequence to make things more interesting.

This exercise can be described as playing the scale in 3rds. Play the first note of the scale (A), skip the next note (B), then play the next note (C#), then go back to the second note of the scale (B), skip the next note (C#) and play the next one (D), and so on.

Expressed in numbers, the sequence looks like this:

1 3, 2 4, 3 5, 4 6, 5 7, 6 8, etc.

Here's that pattern played ascending and descending.

**Example 7g:**

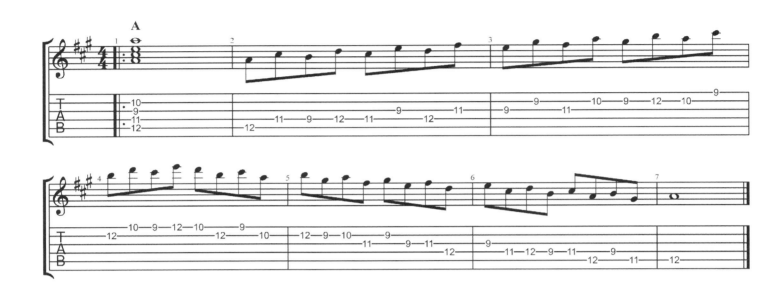

It's also possible to combine sequences. In this example, you will ascend the scale in 3rds, then descend with the descending 4ths pattern.

Breaking out of predictable patterns is the test that separates the men from the boys. You can do this stuff, you just have to *want* to!

**Example 7h:**

Here's the opposite of the last example. Play ascending 4s on the way up, and 3rds on the way down. I've also included an ascending arpeggio at the end to keep you on your toes.

**Example 7i:**

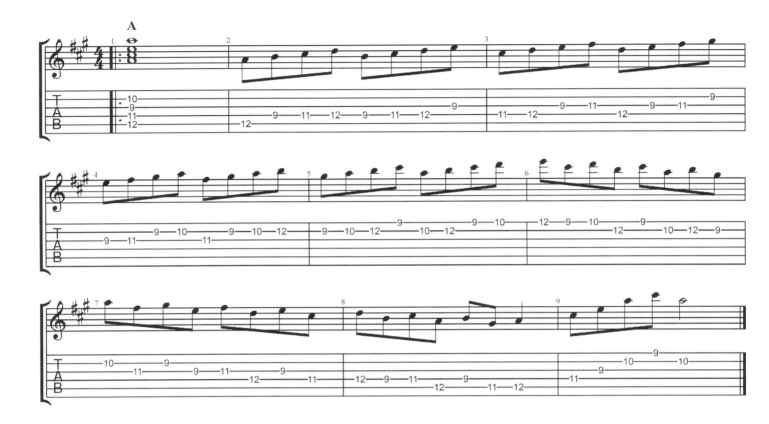

One of my favourite ways to practice scale positions is to ascend an arpeggio and descend the scale. I find this approach sounds more musical, but still presents a technical challenge, as it means moving from picking single notes on each string to playing scalically.

Remember, you should be alternate picking all of this! Get that hand moving before you play and don't let it stop.

**Example 7j:**

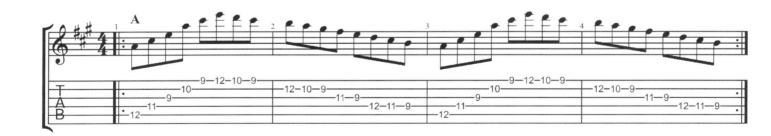

Finally, here's the same idea, but now using the E shape. Can you still remember that position? I hope so!

**Example 7k:**

Good luck, I'll catch you in a week!

# Routine Eight – Legato

For seven solid weeks I've been drilling you in timing, fretboard visualisation, and picking technique, but it's finally time for a break, so that you can start developing your fretting hand strength a bit more. For that, we're going to look at legato technique.

*Legato* means "smoothly" or "connected", but when guitar players use the term they're really talking about using hammer-ons and pull-offs. This technique requires a lot of fretting hand strength, as it involves using that hand to sound the notes most of the time, rather than picking them.

I'm not one of those players who falls into the category of "a legato player" or "a picker". It's not a case of one or the other for me, I just do what I need in order to get the sound I want to hear. So, our goal here isn't to turn you into Joe Satriani or Steve Vai, it's to arm you with a useful technique you can use in your playing when the occasion calls for it.

As you develop some control with this technique, you'll find that you can combine legato fluidly with picked passages to create all manner of sounds. It never hurts to have another option.

The learning objectives here are simple:

* Increase fretting hand dexterity

* Develop legato timing

* Play scales with legato feel

Let's not waste time, here we go!

We'll start our routine by warming up with some hammer-ons. Use your index and ring fingers to play the exercise. Starting on the low E, pick the first not and hammer from fret 1 to 3. Move across the strings until you get to the high E, then move your hand up into the next position and use index and ring fingers to pick then hammer from frets 2 to 4 and move back across the strings. Follow through the exercise to the end.

The aim is for each hammer-on to match the volume of the picked note. This means being fairly forceful with the hammered note, but also make sure you don't pick the notes too loudly, as that will take away from the impact of the legato sound.

**Example 8a:**

The next exercise is similar, but this time uses the index and pinky finger. Other than the wider stretch, it is executed in the same way.

**Example 8b:**

With those two ideas under your belt, let's apply hammer-ons to the A Minor Pentatonic scale, with a fingering that lends itself to legato. When you reach the high E string, shift position up a half step and descend the Bb Minor Pentatonic scale. Next, you'll ascend the B Minor Pentatonic scale and descend Bb Minor Pentatonic.

Notice that we're only dealing with hammer-ons at present. This allows us to focus on playing with good timing, as pull-offs are a little trickier to handle.

**Example 8c:**

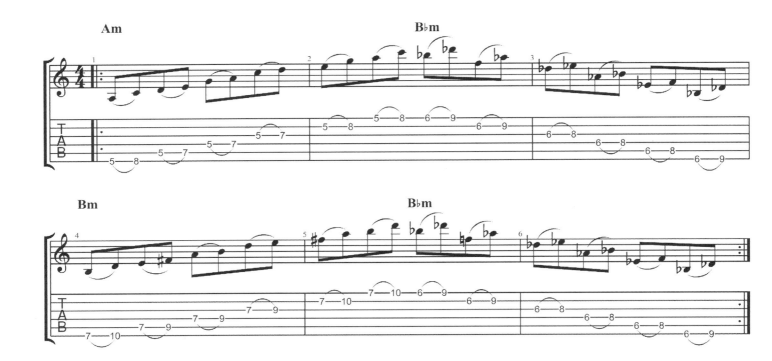

Now it's time to address pull-offs. What makes these trickier is that we have to "pull away" when releasing a fretted note, as the name suggests, not just lift our finger off the string. The finger is actually plucking the strings as it leaves.

I always like to think of it like there's some dirt on the fretboard that you want to brush off as your finger leaves the string.

In this example, pull off from the ring finger to the index with the same pattern seen in Example 8a. You're moving up one position, down the next, up the next, and so on.

**Example 8d:**

Now repeat the same idea but this time with the pinky and index finger.

**Example 8e:**

Now let's apply these pull-offs to the minor pentatonic scale, so you can combine the two fingerings into something more practical.

**Example 8f:**

The next logical step is to combine hammer-ons and pull-offs through the minor pentatonic scale.

Beginning on the G string, hammer on then pull off at the 7th fret, then pick the 7th fret on the D string. After repeating this, move over to the G and B strings and do the same; then the same on the B and E strings.

The second half of the exercise follows the same moves, but now without the repetition, so you're moving between string sets more quickly.

**Example 8g:**

The following example uses more hammer-ons and pull-offs with the minor pentatonic shape. Pay attention to your timing here. You don't have the picking hand swinging away to help keep time here, so you need to produce some solid timing with the fretting hand.

**Example 8h:**

Before we deal with full scales, we need to put a little time into developing some strength between the index and middle fingers. It's likely that you already have a strong bond between these fingers, but let's run through the concept from Example 8a anyway.

**Example 8i:**

Next, we're looking at a longer scale idea. This requires you to play more than two notes on each string. The idea here is to pull off from the pinky finger to the index, then hammer on to a note in between with the middle finger, before pulling back off to the index finger.

This is a nice dexterity exercise, so take it slowly and build up speed over time.

**Example 8j:**

Now let's apply this concept to a three-note-per-string major scale idea. This could be built up to absolutely silly speeds, but our focus here is control and timing over speed. It's also a workout for all four of the fretting hand fingers, so it's a great exercise for balance.

**Example 8k:**

In this example you'll ascend and descend an E shape major scale, but rather than picking all the notes, you'll use your legato technique.

This will be tricky, as you need to combine two and three notes on strings. Make sure your timing is solid here and, whatever happens, don't dig in too hard with the pick when need to sound the strings.

**Example 8l:**

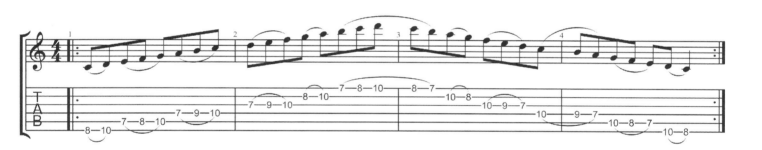

Here's the same idea applied to the C shape major scale that you worked on last week. The same ideas from the last example are relevant here. This is an exercise, not a musical example. Think of it like a morning in the gym. It's good for you!

**Example 8m:**

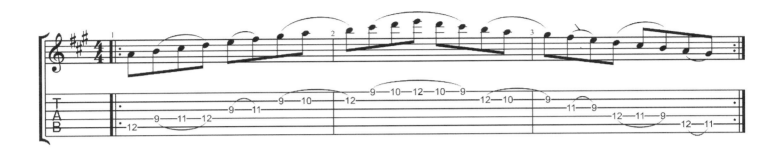

Don't rush through this week, take your time, as these skills will be integral to your long-term development.

Good luck, and I'll see you in a week!

# Routine Nine – A Shape Major Scale

We're nine weeks in and you've probably not even taken a moment to think about how far you've come. We're good at that – so focused on where we're going that we forget where we used to be. At this stage, you should have seen some real progress in your playing, but there's still plenty of time for growth.

This week we're going to round off our major scale knowledge by looking at the A shape fingering. Once you have this down, combine it with all of the sequences and picking patterns we've covered, and you'll have all the tools you'll ever need to play major scales anywhere on the neck.

After working with the A shape, we're going to mix it up with the E and C shapes learned previously.

We're working with our minds a lot here, learning new shapes and sequences, but it's also a great workout for the picking hand. If you want, you can also play this routine legato style too. The beauty of practice routines is that they can be tailored to your specific interests and needs as a player. That's OK, in fact, I encourage it.

The learning objectives for today include:

* A shape major scale

* Application of sequences

* Combining all three major scale patterns

* Developing melodic content


Let's get on with it.

First up we're going to warm up with an alternate picking drill that moves through the E shape major scale in the key of G.

I've written this as an ascending/descending scale, but you could approach it any way you like. Try playing the scale in 3rds or use the ascending 4s pattern. Use whatever you fancy to keep you on your toes.

**Example 9a:**

Now let's review the C shape major scale. This one is probably fresher in your mind as we worked on it extensively just a couple of weeks ago. Again, feel free to mix it up with sequences if this doesn't feel like a challenge for you anymore.

**Example 9b:**

Now we're going to stay in the key of G, play the A shape G major chord, then flesh it out to play the A shape G Major scale.

As this fingering is new, take your time and commit it to memory. You will need to know it automatically if you want to use it to play through sequences and eventually improvise melodies.

**Example 9c:**

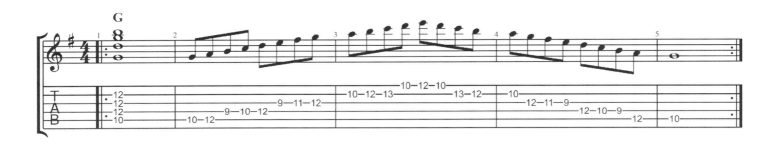

Let's keep ourselves on our toes by changing position, moving down to the key of D at the 5th fret. This shouldn't be much of a problem, you just need to ensure that you are comfortable dealing with the variation in fret distance. Down here the frets are a little further apart and that should be considered.

**Example 9d:**

Now let's look at applying our ascending 4s pattern up and down this major scale in the key of D. While this looks like a long exercise on paper, at this stage your brain should be latching onto the pattern. The more you work with it, the more you'll find you develop the ability to apply the pattern to any scale fingering, rather than viewing it as a long series of notes you need to memorise.

**Example 9e:**

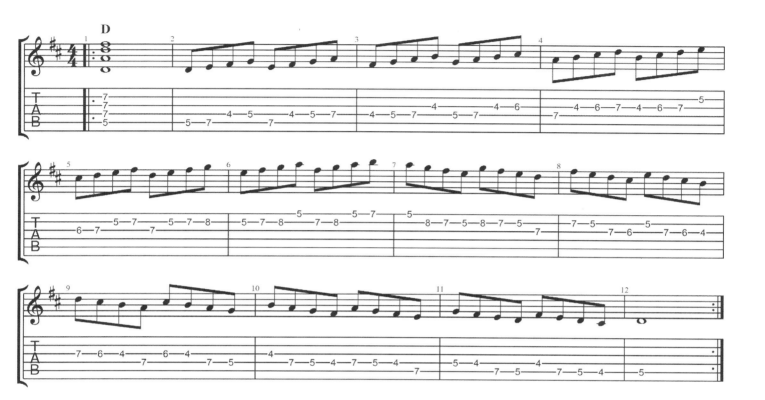

Next up, we'll apply the 3rds pattern to the same scale position. Personally, I'm so comfortable with 3rds that you could hand me an alternate tuned guitar and diagram of a scale I don't know and playing the pattern would still be automatic. Repetition has got me there and you'll get there too, it's just practice.

**Example 9f:**

In the next exercise, we'll ascend the triad arpeggio and descend the scale. The challenge is the same problem as usual: playing just one note on a string as part of a pattern can be tricky, especially at speed. Take this slowly until the motion becomes automatic. Even after playing for 20 years, I'll sometimes trip myself up playing these at speed.

**Example 9g:**

With the three positions programmed in, let's play through A Major, D Major and E Major scales at the 5th fret. Remember our skill of seeing root notes? Ask yourself where the A note is, where D is, and where E is. We can play each of those chords in this position using the E shape for A major, the A shape for D major, and the C shape for E major.

Play the scales starting on the root note over two bars.

**Example 9h:**

In a playing situation, you may not need to play three major scales in quick succession, but you may well want to play the same major scale in several different positions. So, here we're going to play the G Major scale in four places on the neck. First around the E shape at the 3rd fret, then the C shape at the 10th fret starting on the pinky finger, then the A shape at the 10th fret starting on the middle finger, and finally back up in the E shape at the 15th fret.

I love doing things like this as it keeps me sharp. Once you're comfortable with the idea, try it in a few different keys.

**Example 9i:**

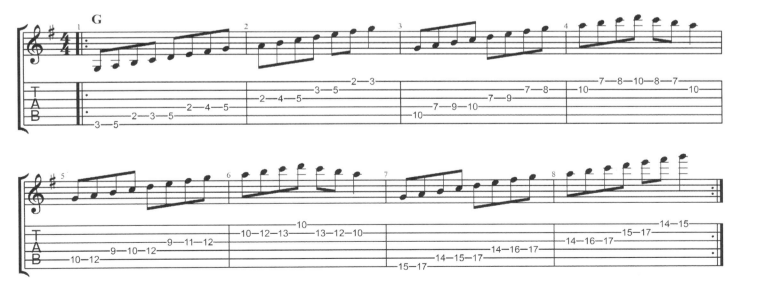

With that scale practice complete, I want to give you some melodic lines to work on that will use your picking skills to execute both scales and arpeggios. Take it slowly at first, but in time you shouldn't have much trouble bringing these up to higher speeds (as long as you've been spending the last nine weeks keeping that picking hand moving!)

**Example 9j:**

Here's another melody in a similar vein to the last, combining scalar ideas with arpeggio movement. Take your time with those arpeggios, they can trip you up if you're not careful.

**Example 9k:**

Our final example is more of a review and preparation for week 10. We're revisiting moving major chords through the Cycle of 4ths, which we looked at in week seven. You'll need to work on this until it's automatic because (spoilers) next week we're going to cycle major scales through this pattern – and that will feel very challenging if you're unprepared.

**Example 91:**

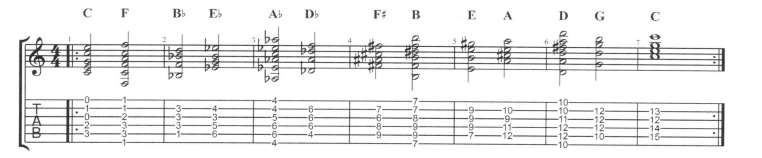

That's all for this week. Repeat this routine as much as you can, but make sure you're just as confident with the scales from previous routines. Remember, there's nothing stopping you going back and redoing earlier routines.

Good luck, and I'll see you in a week.

# Routine Ten – Full Circle & Bends

And here we are at the final routine!

As you might expect, this routine brings together a lot of information from previous routines. With that in mind, expect your struggles to be a direct reflection of how much work you've put in to this point. If you find yourself hitting a wall, don't be afraid to dial things back and return to work on previous routines. Becoming great on your instrument isn't a race, it's a journey.

This week we're going to use all of our chord shapes, rhythm skills and picking skills; we'll play scales around the full Circle of 4ths, and use legato technique; then we're going to introduce bends to finish off.

Bends feel like a good place to end, as they're one of the techniques that make the guitar unique. It's not possible to manipulate pitch when playing the piano, for example, and bending strings is one of the best ways to bring out the vocal quality of the guitar. It demands some technical considerations, but time working on it will be time well spent.

This book has not been about teaching you techniques (there are plenty of books available which are dedicated to that) but here's one tip for when you get to the bending section: remember that bending strings doesn't come from the fingers moving. We don't have enough strength or control to execute that movement with the fingers alone. The movement comes from locking the fingers in place and turning the forearm, just like turning a key in a door. You'll have much more power and control when doing it like this. The thumb will be higher up on the neck, potentially even over the top of the neck. Give your technique a critical check when you get to that part!

We'll begin with the original 1234 chromatic style warm-up, but this time played with legato technique. Since the pick is doing less work here, the timing has to come from the fretting hand, not the picking hand. Focus on the timing so that you don't rush or drag. Also, don't pick the first note on each string too hard, so that the volume of the notes remains consistent throughout.

Moving forward, you can apply legato technique to any of the chromatic style warm-up patterns or finger permutations we've covered.

**Example 10a:**

The next two examples will combine some of our chordal knowledge with rhythms and then scales.

The first example uses the progression from the soul tune, *Let's Get It On*.

We're playing F major with the C shape, then A minor, Bb major and C major with the E shape. Notice that we're applying the Charleston rhythm to the progression.

These chords all belong to the key of F Major, so if you wanted to solo over them, the F Major scale would be a good place to start.

This isn't a book on improvisation, but visualisation is the first step on the way to it. Being able to see how scales are located around chords is an important skill to work on.

**Example 10b:**

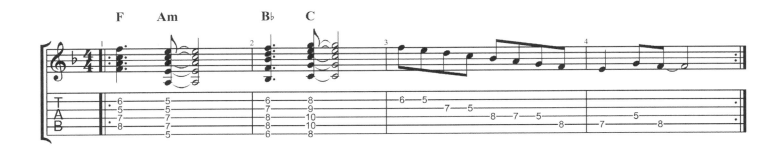

The next example is based on the chord progression to *Signed, Sealed, Delivered*. The chords are similar, but now we've added a D minor chord using the A shape and some more interesting rhythms.

Once again, your goal here is to be able to visualise the F Major scale and how it fits around the chords. You're using the C shape for the major scale, but if the chords were played in a different position, you'd need to visualise a different scale pattern.

**Example 10c:**

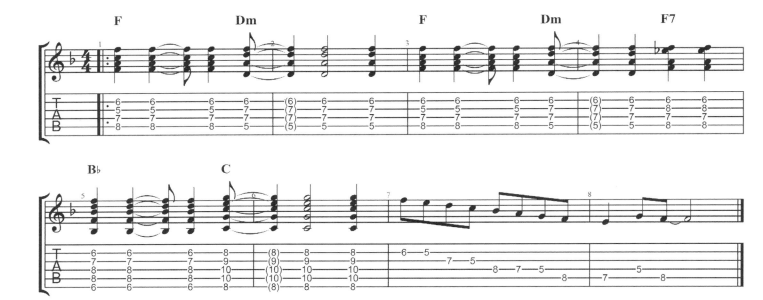

In a minute we'll practice the major scale using the Cycle of 4ths, but before we do, let's review the chords in order once more. You can probably do this now without having to think about the chords very much, but make an effort to say the chord names out loud as you play them. Embed this progression into memory and train it into your fingers.

C – F – Bb – Eb – Ab – Db – F# – B – E – A – D – G – C

**Example 10d:**

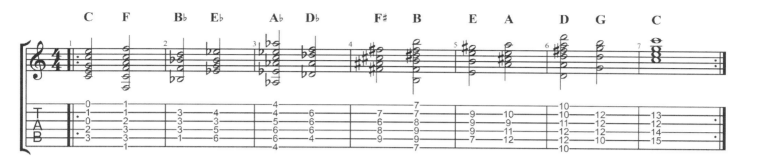

Now we're going to play major scales in all 12 keys using the root note/position roadmap from the previous example.

First up we'll do this starting on the root note and playing the scale in one octave, ascending.

**Example 10e:**

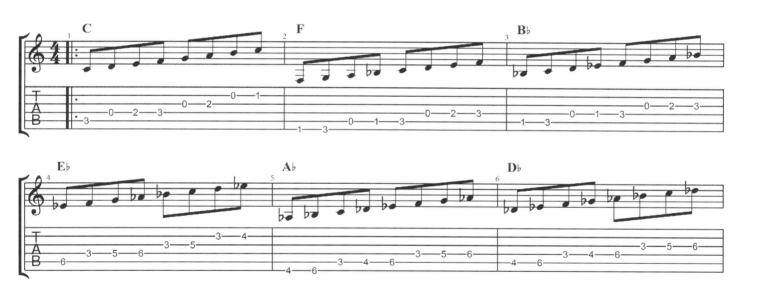

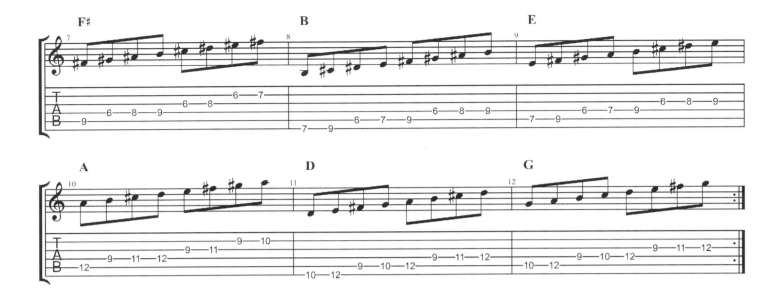

Now play the same scales in the same positions, but start on the higher root note and descend an octave.

**Example 10f:**

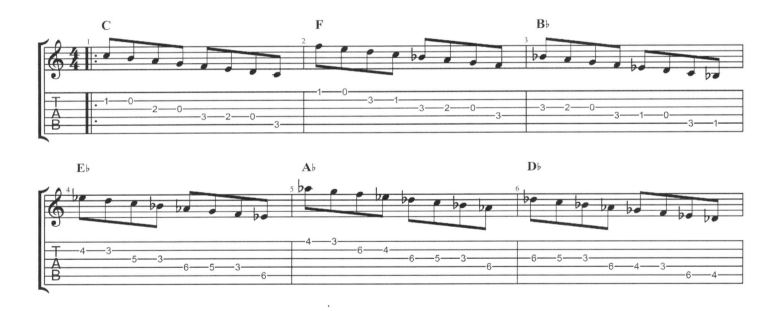

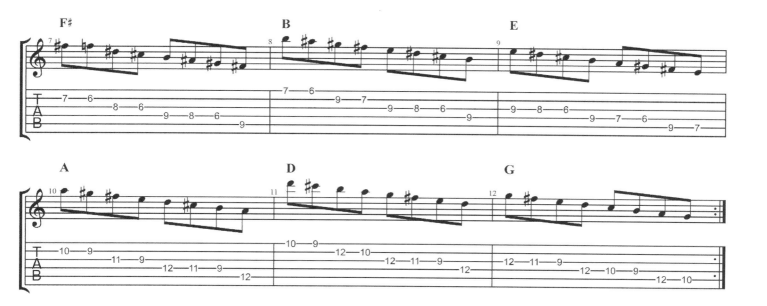

Now it's time to work on some bends to complete the routine.

In this exercise you'll play the 7th fret on the G string (D), bend this note up a whole step to E, then play the note E on the 5th fret of the B string. This will allow you to check the accuracy of your bend. Make sure you're bending perfectly to an E note. The bent note and the fretted note should sound exactly the same.

Do this twice, then repeat the exercise on the B and high E strings.

**Example 10g:**

Bending accuracy is the most important thing to focus on here, as this will make your playing sound controlled and expression comes from control.

The following example is based around the A Minor Pentatonic scale. You're bending the higher note on each string up to the next note in the scale to create a melody, so focus on that accuracy.

**Example 10h:**

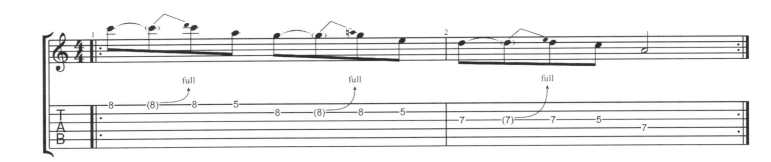

Your bends don't have to be limited to the minor pentatonic scale. The following example uses all the notes of the major scale. You'll play a melody that is picked (B, C, B), then play the same thing by bending up and releasing. Then do the same on the next note down (A, B, A) then with bends; then the next note (G, A, G) and then with bends, and so on.

**Example 10i:**

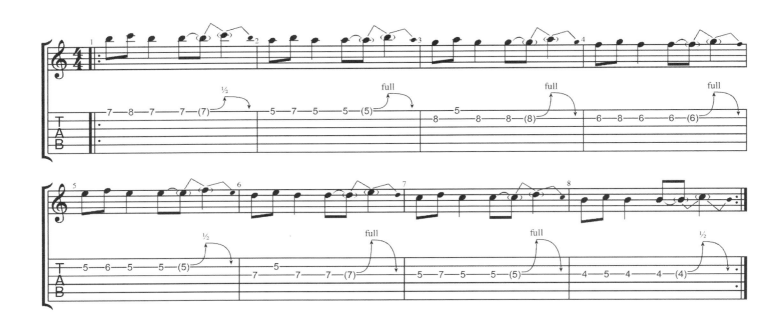

Out final four examples are all licks rather than straight exercises. The idea here is to apply bends to the pentatonic scale to create a classic blues rock sound. These can be played as fast or as slow as you like – the focus should be on making sure your bends are accurate and your timing is good.

The first lick features bends and cross picking. I've seen players attempt to work out ways to pick this, to make it easier, but the truth is, if your alternate picking is solid, you won't find it a problem.

**Example 10j:**

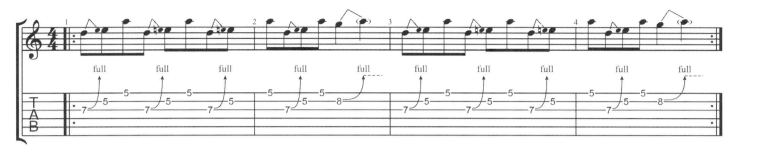

The next idea uses similar bends and picking patterns, but now you'll add some legato to connect your notes.

You may also spot the Eb note in the penultimate bar. That's the "blue" note from the blues scale, but we'll learn more about that in the future!

**Example 10k:**

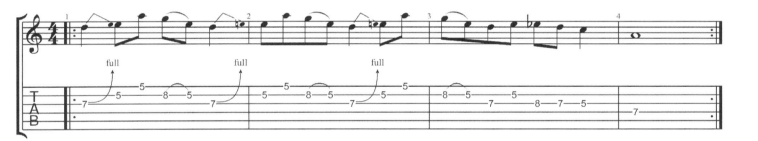

The following lick only bends one note. The challenge here is smoothly combining picking and legato. This might feel easy when played slowly, but all these ideas are designed to be played fast. Think Angus Young or Jimmy Page, or if you want to go faster, Alvin Lee or Frank Marino.

**Example 10l:**

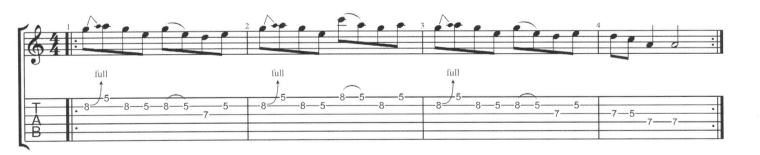

The final lick is a little longer with less repetition and includes bends of both a tone and a semitone. This one has more of the flavour of Eric Johnson or Joe Bonamassa. That should give you an idea of the long-term speed goal for something like this.

**Example 10m:**

And that's it, the final routine, done! Get to work on this, then come back for the conclusion. You're far from done, so don't relax just yet.

# Conclusion

There you go, you did it!

It may have seemed a long 10 weeks, but you've made it through, and I'd imagine you're a significantly better player than when you started.

You have a bunch of options now (the most obvious one being to take a week off, then get on with the next book!)

To wrap up, I want to talk here about your needs. We done these practice routines together, but my long-term goal is for you to *not* need me. As you develop your playing, you should become confident in creating your own practice routines, designed with your own specific needs in mind.

One approach is to review all the material we've covered, then chop up the routines to create your own custom routine. Maybe the area you need to work on is scales; maybe it's just chords. You're in charge.

Consider your needs, but also your personal circumstances.

I designed these routines to be around 10 minutes long, but if you have more time available, make longer routines. In the early stages, as with these foundational exercises, shorter routines make more sense, but more advanced players will probably want to put in more time.

If you're lucky enough to play music for a living, the chances are you'll have more spare time to put into it. If you happen to have kids, time might be limited. Make sure the routines you create are realistic for your lifestyle, but at the same time, don't be afraid to push yourself a little.

This is just the beginning of what you need to become that bulletproof musician. There's still much ground to cover, including minor scales, modes, 7th chords and arpeggios, position shifting, sweep/economy picking, tapping, reading, fingerstyle and more! The list goes on, but you've armed yourself with a great start here, both physically, and philosophically.

Good luck with your practice. I wish you all the luck in overcoming yourself and finding that love for getting better on your instrument.

Until next time!

*Levi.*

Made in the USA
Las Vegas, NV
04 August 2023

75644383R00048